Young Kings

I Came from Greatness

Color Me Beautiful

Sha Sekhmet Ankh Maat

Library of Congress Control Number:		2022921290
ISBN:	Softcover	978-1-6698-5571-2
	eBook	978-1-6698-5570-5

Print information available on the last page.

Rev. date: 11/11/2022

To order additional copies of this book, contact:
Xlibris
844-714-8691
www.Xlibris.com
Orders@Xlibris.com
848365

This book belongs to

Your Name

Our Ancestors are always watching over us.

I Love My Family

The Ankh is the Egyptian symbol of Life!

Mansa Musa
was the Richest
African King
in Timbukto-Mali

Help The King Find His Queen

This is a MER! The Greeks renamed it, Pyramid. The Pyramids were built by African Egyptians around 2700 B.C.E. (before common era)

Taharqa was a Pharoah (King) of Ancient Egypt and Ethiopia.

2 Kings 19:9

8

Hannibal, the Greatest African Military General.

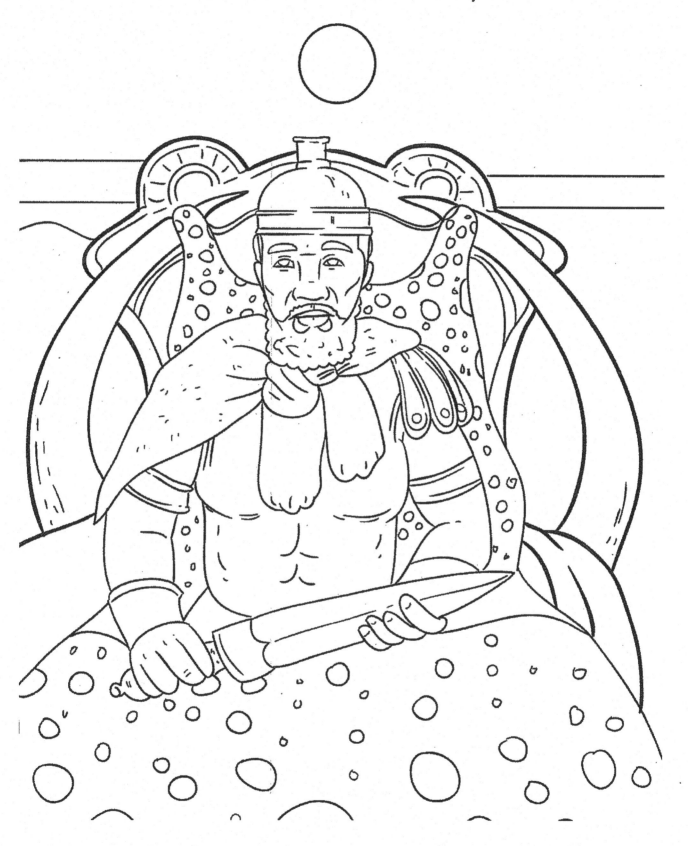

King Tut-Ankh-Amun

10

Thutmose III
was the sixth Pharaoh of
the 18th Dynasty

This is a SanKofa symbol from Ghana,
Africa It means "Go back and get it".

Africa is the Motherland of Humanity!

A_____is the M_____of H_____

God and Goddess of Ancient Egypt

Ausar and Auset

African King

Africa is Beautiful

We Love To Learn

I Love to play
the
Drum!

19

The Kundi harp is an arched instrument that comes from Central Africa! It is a sweet sounding instrument played during ceremonies and celebrations! All began in Africa!

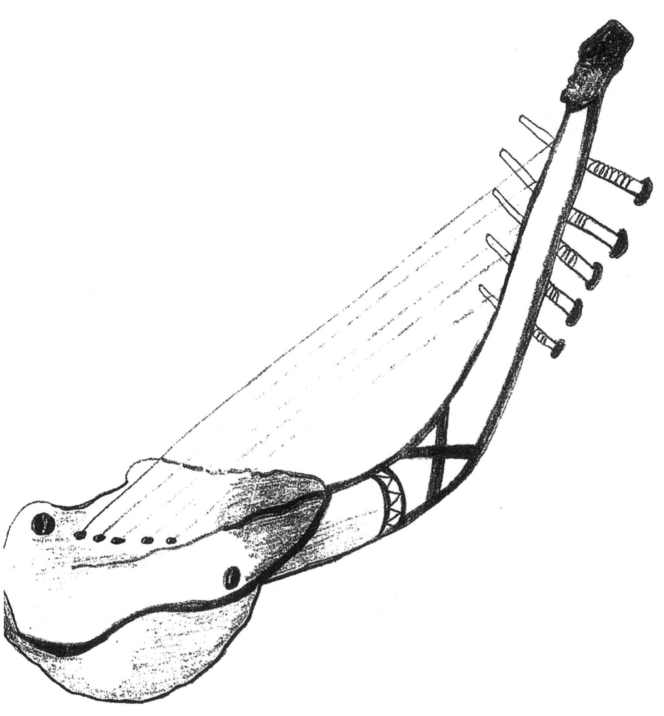

Its Fun to Ride my Bike!

Africa had many Queens and Kings!

Queen Nandi, Mother of King Shaka
Zulu, was from South Africa.

Shaka Zulu
Son of Queen Nandi, Was a King
with a powerful Army in South Africa.

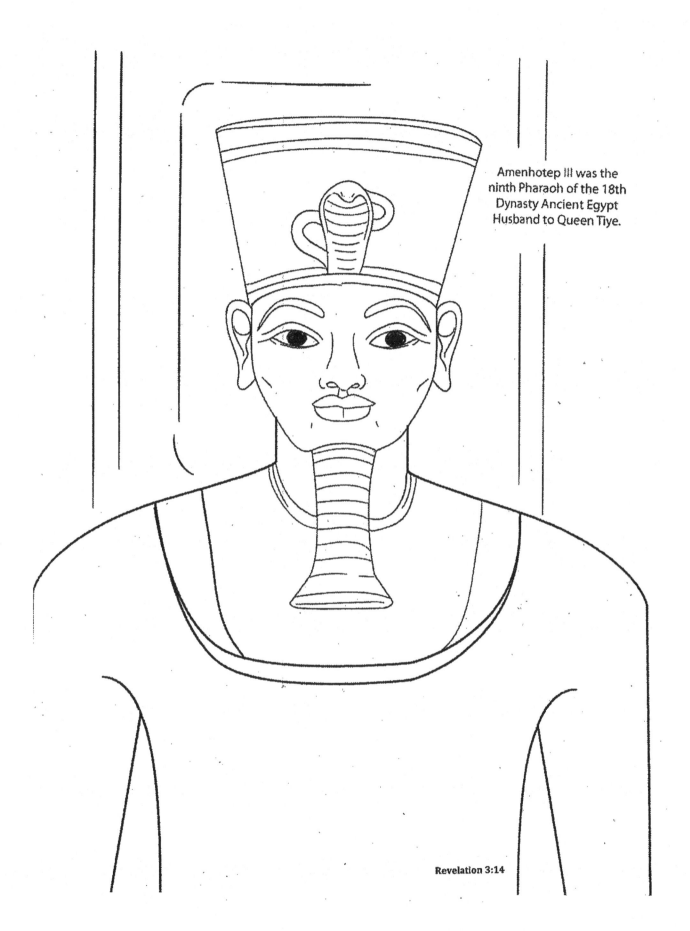

Amenhotep III was the ninth Pharaoh of the 18th Dynasty Ancient Egypt Husband to Queen Tiye.

Revelation 3:14

We Love To Share!

How many words can you find?

```
I  A  B  C  Z  I  K  L  I  K
C  S  R  Q  X  A  B  H  M  I
D  K  I  S  S  U  N  E  O  N
G  I  O  S  P  S  G  R  T  G
H  N  C  Y  H  E  R  U  E  Q
Z  G  E  H  I  T  E  M  P  U
D  E  K  U  N  I  A  N  L  E
L  N  T  N  X  Z  T  O  Y  E
A  F  R  I  C  A  E  P  Q  N
B  P  Y  R  A  M  I  D  P  Z
K  E  M  E  T  E  G  Y  P  T
```

ISIS		AFRICA
KING		ANKH
SPHINX		HERU
AUSET		PYRAMID
SUN	QUEEN	IMOTEP
GREAT	EGYPT	KEMET

I COME FROM GREATNESS!

REWRITE

I_____ _____G_____!

27

I Love To Dance.

Imhotep was the first Doctor in
Ancient Kemet (Egypt)
He was also an Architect and Astronomer.

The Scarab Beetle
represents Renewal

Write down which number comes next in the sequence!

1). 1, 2, 3, 4, ____, 6, 7.

2). 2, 4, 6, 8, ____, 12, 14.

3). 3, 6, ____, 12, 15, 18, 21.

4). 5, 10, 15, 20, ____, 30, 35.

5). 40, 45, 50, ____, 60, 65, 70.

6). 10, 20, 30, ____, 50, 60, 70.

You did a Wonderful job!

Learning is Fun!

Match each letter to the picture with
the same beginning sound.

K

P

B

A

Q

C

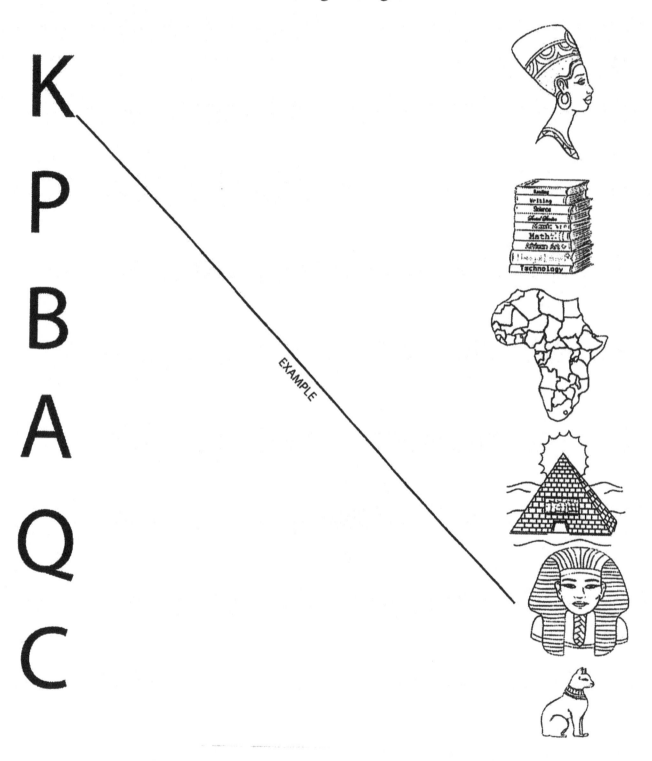

EXAMPLE

Your Name_____

There are 54 countries in Africa
Name and color each one!

Mediterranean Sea

Gulf of Guinea

Indian Ocean

Atlantic Ocean

Add and Match To The Correct Answer:

Akhenaten was Pharaoh of Ancient Egypt and
was crowned Amenhotep IV

Count and Match to the Correct Number

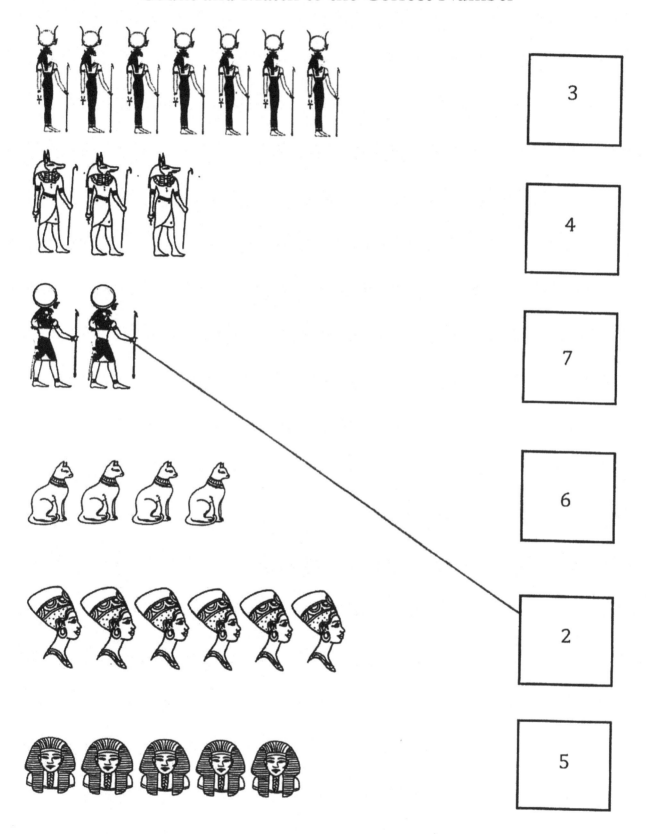

The Drum came from Africa! It is a very important Instrument during ceremonies and celebrations!

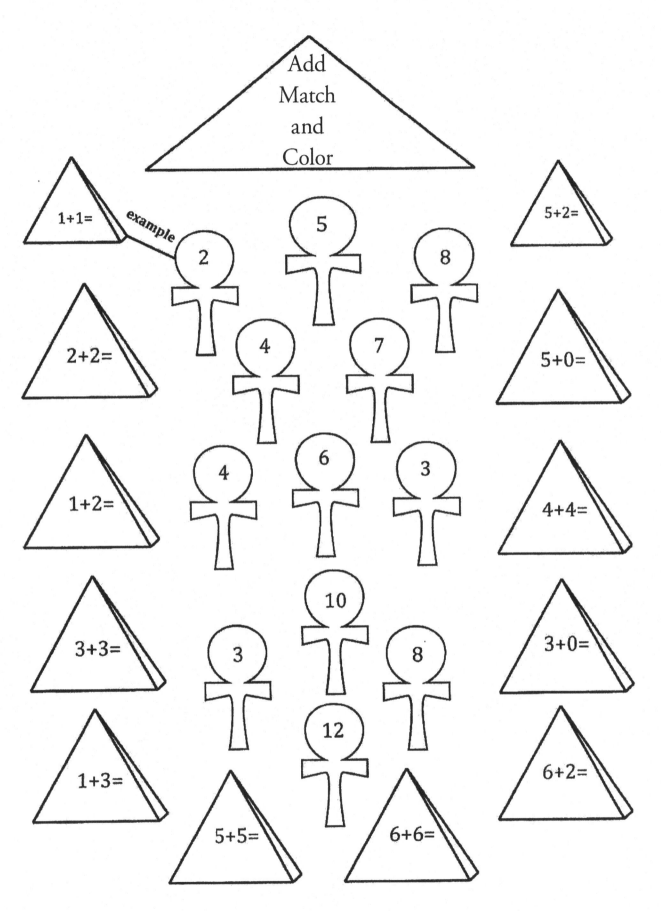

Add
Match
and
Color

1+1=   *example*

5+2=

5

2   8

4   7   5+0=

2+2=

1+2=   4   6   3   4+4=

10

3+3=   3   8   3+0=

12

1+3=   6+2=

5+5=   6+6=

Subtract
Match
and
Color

3-1=

1

1

2-1=

2

4-3=

3

5

6-3=

4

5-2=

8

6

6-2=

7

8-2=

9-1=

7-2=

8-1=

Color Your African Mask!

Count the objects in each box then match
them to the correct number.

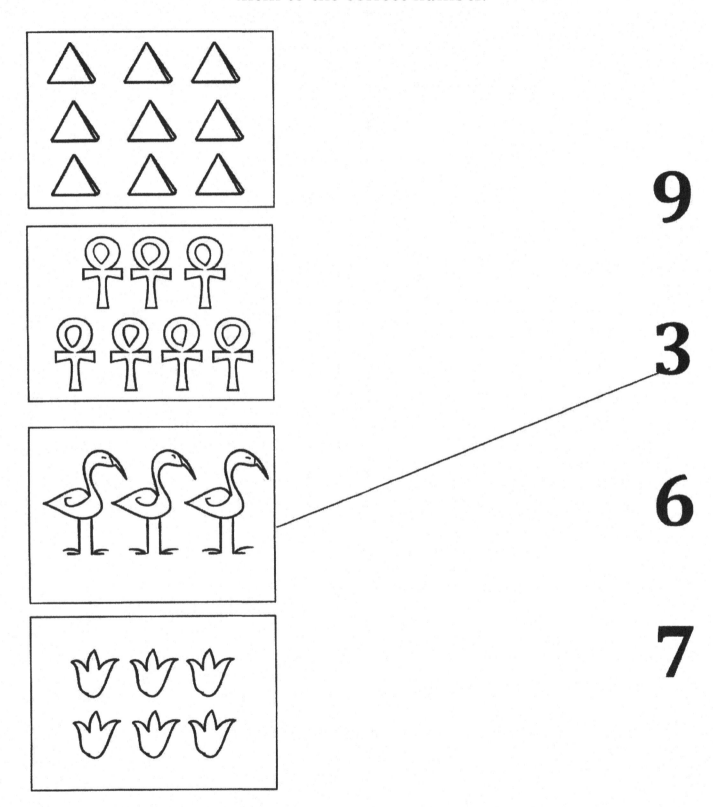

9

3

6

7

Please help him find his reading book.

Beautiful Animals Come From Africa!
The Lion!

Elephants are Beautiful

In Africa they have large Buffalo

The obelisk, better known as the Tekenhu was created in Egypt!
Many have taken and copied the obelisk, it can be seen all over the
world. In Washington D.C. it is called Washington Monument.
But it originally came from Egypt which is in Africa!

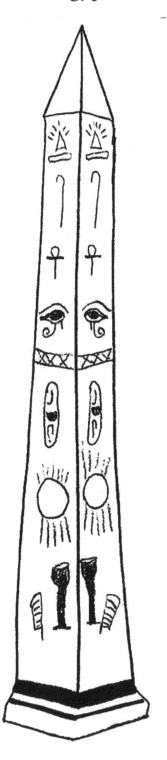

Mother Africa!
Mother of Humanity!

The Universe

Sirius Star

Moon

Earth

Our Grandparents are to be honored with
respect always just like our parents.

Printed in the United States
by Baker & Taylor Publisher Services